REACTIONS
ARE
SHOWING

by J. Allan Petersen

Director of Family Concern, Inc.

BACK TO THE BIBLE®

Copyright © 1967
by
The Good News Broadcasting Association, Inc.
All rights reserved.

460,000 printed to date—1996
(1160-192—5M—46)
ISBN 978-0-8474-0999-0

Printed in the United States of America

Foreword

J. Allan Petersen is the director of Family Concern, Inc.—a concerted contemporary effort to strengthen home and marriage and to encourage successful partnership, competent parenthood and meaningful family life.

The first three chapters of this booklet were previously published in the *Good News Broadcaster* (now *Confident Living*), Back to the Bible's magazine for adults. We later decided to combine those chapters with the others in a pocket-size booklet. We trust God will use them in this form with increasing blessing in the lives of His people.

—The Publishers

Contents

Chapter 1

Revealing and Ruinous Reactions

Much of our Christian teaching has been occupied with right actions. We have been taught: "Do this, for it is right; but don't do that, because it is wrong." Right actions are important. The Bible speaks clearly concerning right things and wrong things. God's Word, though it is not a book of negatives, does declare that certain actions are evil in themselves. From these we must refrain.

The Bible also gives us commissions and commands. We are just as obligated to obey God in those as we are to refrain from what He has forbidden. We all know that wrong actions can be ruinous. They can adversely affect one's personality and bring defeat into his life. But do we realize that wrong reactions can hurt us as much as wrong actions—perhaps even more so? What is more, wrong reactions can be found in people whose actions on the surface are correct and proper. A person who prides himself on his right actions might truthfully say, "I don't lie, I don't cheat, I don't swear, I don't get drunk, I don't commit adultery." His actions are correct and proper, yet he may be utterly defeated by his wrong reactions to life's situations and other people's actions.

We may at any given moment pride ourselves on right actions and yet be reacting with jealousy, or resentment, or anger, or hatred, or fear or self-pity. To react in one or several of these ways when things do not please us will be very harmful to us.

Were a person to watch my actions, he would not really know me. My actions would not reveal to him what I really am, because my actions might be planned and practiced for his benefit. But it is our reactions—our spontaneous, un-

conscious, unscheduled reactions—
that reveal what we really are.

For instance, a child is playing
all alone in his playpen enjoying his
toys. As we observe him, we think,
"He is a happy and contented
child." Actually, we do not know
anything about him by watching
him under these circumstances. But
bring another small child into that
playpen and let him reach out for
one of those toys, and we may see a
radical change in the first child. We
may see a reaction of anger expressed by a scream of resentment.
Selfishness comes to the surface
and the reaction reveals what is in
the heart of the child. It is not so
much our actions that reveal what
we are but our unplanned reactions.

What are our car-driving reactions? How do we react as we
move around in traffic? Some
persons keep up a steady stream of
comment and advice concerning
each driver they meet on the road.
If someone makes a mistake in
traffic, it bothers them so that they
react strongly—sometimes even
expressing themselves forcefully.

Just a short time ago I saw a man roll down his car window and yell at another driver. Here was a decided reaction, and the reaction revealed what was inside the man.

A young person goes off to college where he is exposed to some knowledge and education. Then, when he returns home, he looks down on people who have not had this privilege. His reaction to his education reveals the kind of person he really is.

Consider some basic factors concerning our reactions—factors which show us how to understand our reactions and what to do about them. First of all, we need to know that in a nonchristian world we are going to be treated in unchristian ways. There will be unchristian actions. It is not difficult to have Christian reactions when things are pleasant and favorable. But when we are treated in unchristian ways, it is easy to have unchristian reactions. The Apostle Peter warned that certain people may speak evil of any who turn to Christ and run no longer with their former companions to the same excess of riot. The Apostle John said in I John 3:13, "Marvel not, my brethren, if the world hate you." And our Lord said in John 15:18, "If the world hate you, ye know that it hated me before it hated you."

What do men find to criticize in Jesus Christ? How could there be unchristian actions toward Christ when His every thought was love and virtually every act was kindness? Yet, He was severely criticized. At times He was bitterly resented; at other times He was openly hated. His reactions to such unchristian treatment, of course, were pure and holy. But since He was mistreated, it should come as no surprise to us who are sinners by nature if we are treated in unchristian ways. We ought never to be shocked at any treatment we receive from anyone. Let us mark that down. It should come as no surprise to us when people are selfish in dealing with us or when they are unkind or critical or resentful.

I think we often play the game of life in a reverse manner. We are

11

always shocked by what happens to us and are unprepared for it. If we believed the Bible, we would know that we will be treated in unchristian ways. We would also know what our reactions should be. We would be prepared and strengthened by our Lord ahead of time, so that our reactions would be right, positive, mature and spiritual.

Our Lord himself was filled with the Spirit; then He was led into the wilderness to be tempted by the Devil. There was both a strengthening and a preparation ahead of time for the temptation that was certain to come. Then, when the temptation did come, His reactions were positive. He did not waver. His reactions were strong. They were mature and spiritual. He was prepared ahead of time.

Most of Christ's ill treatment came from religious people. That is something to remember. Have we not found this to be true also? Religious people and even Christian people can be unkind, unethical, critical, dishonest, quarrelsome and bitter. Thus we know what actions may be expected.

The questions we need to ask ourselves are such as these: Do we know what our reaction should be? Are we prepared ahead of time for the actions we know are coming so that we will react as Christ wants us to react?

This brings us to the second factor concerning reactions. Do we realize that our reactions reveal our true selves? I cannot react in any manner contrary to what I really am. My nature is revealed by my reactions. The Prophet Jeremiah states, "The heart is deceitful above all things, and desperately wicked" (Jer. 17:9). Isaiah said, "All we like sheep have gone astray; we have turned every one to his own way; and the Lord hath laid on him the iniquity of us all" (Isa. 53:6). God says that we must see our basic nature is deceitful and selfish. We are a self-centered people. We want our own way. Since this is our natural tendency, this is what will be revealed by our reactions. It is always easy to say, and we will either say it or think it when we react in an unkind, unchristian manner, "Well, you know, it is really not like me to act in that way." Or we might say, "Don't judge me by that isolated instance, I am really better than I appear to be; that is really not a true expression of my character."

Have you ever felt that way? Of course you have and so have I. The opposite is true, however, for our reactions reveal what we really are inside.

Suppose we take a tea bag and drop it into a cup of hot water. As we watch it we will see a dark-brown color flow from that bag until the entire cup of hot water is dark brown. How foolish to look at that color and say, "I know it looks dark brown, and everyone would think it was dark brown, but I won't believe it. I would rather say that it is a beautiful shade of pink, even though I know it is not."

And how foolish to take a lemon, squeeze it and declare that the sour juice squeezed from it was sweet—even though we knew it was

14

not. Honesty would demand we admit the juice to be sour. So does personal honesty demand that we admit what we really are.

Have we ever been in "hot water"? Have we been in hot water with a husband? Or wife? Or children? Or relatives? How did we react? How did we respond? Like the dark-brown color that comes from the tea bag, something unchristian shows up in our reactions. We cannot blame someone else for putting that into us. The truth is, he or she merely brought out what was dominant in us at that moment. The hot water did not put the color in the tea bag. It brought the color out. Squeezing a lemon does not make the juice bitter or sour. So this is what our reactions do. They reveal what is already in us.

When we react in the wrong way to something or some person, we confirm what our Lord said in Mark 7:20-23: "That which cometh out of the man, that defileth the man. For from within, out of the heart of men, proceed evil thoughts, adulteries, fornications, murders, thefts, covetousness, wickedness, deceit, lasciviousness, an evil eye, blasphemy, pride, foolishness: all these evil things come from within, and defile the man.''

That is why we cannot blame the pressure built up by a problem for the way we react. We can never honestly blame the difficulty for the wrong things we say or do. God says that the situation does not put these things into us, it merely brings out what is already in our nature.

This is one of the secrets of spiritual growth. If God shows me by my reactions that I am a very critical person, and I admit it to Him and begin to deal with it, then I will grow spiritually. The Spirit of God will cause me to become a more mature believer. This, however, demands a great amount of personal honesty.

Chapter 2

Who Controls You?

If we react in the same manner that other persons act toward us, those persons control us. Paul said in Romans 12:17, "Recompense to no man evil for evil." He stated the same truth in I Thessalonians 5:15 where he said, "See that none render evil for evil unto any man." The same principle is laid down by Peter: "Not rendering evil for evil, or railing for railing: but contrariwise blessing" (I Pet. 3:9).

All these passages say the same thing. They tell us not to react the same way people act toward us. If someone acts toward us in an evil manner, God says we are not to be guilty of reacting in an evil manner.

Suppose I walk down a street and a stranger comes up to me and without any word or reason hits me

17

in the face. That, you would agree, is wrong. He is guilty of a wrong action, and by doing it he reveals his hostility toward me. He ought to make amends for such a wrong action.

But suppose I hit him back? I do to him what he did to me—what is that? A wrong reaction! That would make me as guilty as he of wrongdoing. My reaction would reveal my hatred toward him as much as his action revealed his hatred toward me. If this were actually to take place, I would have to acknowledge that the man controlled me.

The meeting was for only a moment or two, yet he controlled me by what he did. He hit me; I hit him back. His action determined my reaction, thus he controlled me. When I reacted in the way he acted, I was in effect saying to him, "I am just like you. I am no better than you. I am as defeated as you. I have the same spirit and disposition that moves you. I will do anything you will do."

Who controls us? How many persons control us? If we react the way others act toward us, they control us. Someone flares up at us and we flare up in return. That person controlled us. Or somebody criticizes us and we return the criticism. We have let that person control us. The actions of others have determined what our reactions will be. When this is the case, we are controlled by everyone we meet. Is not that a tragedy? We have the life of children of God so that we should be exhibiting right reactions, yet so often we are controlled by those around us.

As I travel across the country in evangelistic work, I find at times one church group or denomination saying, "We won't have anything to do with that other group. Even though we both love the Lord and are members of the Body of Christ, we are going to scratch them off our list." Then the other group responds, "If that is your decision, then we'll scratch you off our list." Thus each group controls the other by their actions and reactions.

One preacher reacts strongly to another preacher and writes a scathing letter to him. The second preacher then retaliates with a letter of the same kind. Here again, two persons are controlled by each other. They are both defeated at the same level.

Church business meetings can be very interesting, to say the least. If one person stands up in the business meeting and says something in anger or bitterness, someone else is likely to respond in the same way. Angry and bitter words beget angry and bitter words. The person who reacts in that way is controlled by the person who acted that way in the first place. How many people control us in our daily experiences?

First Peter 3 deals with family relations. It speaks of a wife and her unsaved husband—how she is supposed to react toward him. The passage also speaks of a husband's reactions toward his wife. It tells him how to deal with her as the weaker vessel.

As a wife, what is your reaction toward your husband? Does he control you? Does his mood determine what your mood will be? If he is upset do you become upset, proving that he controls you? If he becomes thoughtless and negligent of you, do you in turn become thoughtless and negligent of him? Then he controls you.

God wants to enable Christians to always have right actions and reactions. Regardless of what other people do to us, we have the strength in Christ to act and react in positive, spiritual ways.

One woman said to me not long ago, "My husband absolutely controls me. When he leaves the house in the morning to go to work, he says the one thing that he knows will upset me. He controls me by this one sentence. Whenever he doesn't want to face something himself, he'll just say this to me and it upsets me all day long. What shall I do?"

I told her, "Your husband is wrong for his action; but you are wrong for your reaction. His action

21

makes him guilty; your reaction makes you guilty. You cannot wait for your husband to say, 'Well, I'll change my action.' You must draw strength from Christ so that you can change your reaction even though your husband does not change his action. You dare not live under the control of anyone else but Jesus Christ."

Husband, does your wife control you? Does her attitude some mornings decide what your attitude will be? Does her wrong action determine your equally wrong re-action so that you decide your conduct by what she has done? If so, she controls you.

I have seen little children control their parents. If it were not so sad it would be humorous. I remember in one home that a little five-year-old boy became angry with one of his parents. He spat out a word of anger. What did the parent do? Exactly what the boy did—spat out an angry word. The child controlled the parent. The child determined by his action what the parent was going to do.

22

It did not end there. The child became angrier and raised his voice and said something a little bit stronger. And the parent? He also raised his voice and said something stronger. An adult was controlled by a child.

Finally the little fellow stamped his tiny foot and declared what he was going to do and what he was not going to do. What was the parent's reaction? He brought his big foot down noisily and said, "No. This is what you are going to do!" The small child's actions determined the parent's reactions.

What a tragedy! The parent had no inner control. He did not know how to speak in a kindly, Christian way and mean what he said. The child did not learn that when his parents spoke they meant what they said—even when they spoke kindly.

The Christian must be controlled by Jesus Christ alone. We cannot do this in ourselves. But under God, through the strength of Christ and controlled by the Spirit, we can initiate right spiritual reactions regardless of what other people's actions have been.

The Apostle Paul said that God will enable us to do this. He wrote: "I can do all things through Christ which strengtheneth me" (Phil. 4:13). The Lord Jesus Christ can strengthen us to have the right reactions to whatever actions we face today. Trust Him, believe Him and keep on believing. God will prove that what He says is true, and He will make us victors in every situation.

Chapter 3

Only Our Reactions Can Hurt Us

Nothing can hurt us except our reactions. This is a most important fact to grasp.

The Bible says in Romans 8:28: "And we know that all things work together for good to them that love God, to them who are the called according to his purpose." This means that it makes no difference what happens if we really believe that everything God allows in our lives is working for our good. In that case, whatever happens makes a contribution to our lives. There is a sense in which we have no enemies. A situation is not our enemy. A problem or difficulty is not an enemy. No, all of these things work together for our good. All are our friends—provided that we are thankful and have the right reaction to them. If our reaction to what happens is not right, then, of course, our reaction will hurt us.

I stood by the bedside of a woman who had had 25 operations. In spite of all that medical science had tried to do for her, she was wasting away. I said to her very kindly, "You surely have had more than your share of suffering. I don't know how I might react in your circumstance, but the truth is that these operations have not hurt you. Even if you had to undergo many more, they still would not hurt you."

She looked up at me in amazement and said, "What do you mean, they couldn't hurt me?"

I answered, "The surgery in itself will not hurt you, but your reaction to your physical problem may hurt you. If you react with bitterness, that bitterness will harm you."

She replied, "Yes, I know what you mean. I know what you mean, now."

Our reactions must be right. The situation that God allows does not hurt us. Instead, it will help if our reactions to it are mature and spiritual and proper. Do you think Helen Keller was hurt because she was blind? Was Beethoven hurt because he was deaf? Was Thomas Edison hurt because he only had three months of schooling? Was Job, the Old Testament patriarch, hurt because he lost what he had?

Was Abraham Lincoln hurt because he was raised in poverty? Was Paul the apostle hurt because he had a thorn in his flesh? Through it he learned more about the grace of God. The thorn in his flesh was a blessing to him.

Was John the apostle hurt when he was exiled to the Island of Patmos because of his faith? No, that did not hurt him. He returned with the Book of the Revelation in his hand. No one can hurt a man like that! No matter what happens to him, he embraces it and says, "God is using this to make me a better person, so I am grateful to Him!" Because his reactions are right he is helped not hurt.

27

other hand, if our re-
wrong—if we react with
—that resentment will
us. If we react with bitterness,
that bitterness will blight us. If we
react with self-pity, that self-pity
will defeat us. If we react with
anger and hatred, they may result
in ulcers or other bodily ills.

How do we react to our home
problems? Some have very serious
home problems. How have we
reacted to difficulties? To temptations? What our reactions have been
will determine if we have been hurt.

Equally important to this sub-
ject is the fact that we are responsible for all our reactions. Our
tendency is to say, "The other
person's actions were so wrong that
we cannot be blamed for our
reactions."

It must be admitted that others
are guilty of wrong actions, but the
Bible says that we are responsible
for our wrong reactions. In writing
to the Thessalonians Paul said, "See
that none render evil for evil"
(I Thess. 5:15). In that little word
"see" lies our responsibility. The

28

Lord says in effect, "Take it upon yourself to be responsible for your reactions; make sure that you don't react the way other people act toward you." This is one of our greatest problems. We do not want to take responsibility. We know that our reactions have been wrong and that they reveal what we really are. In our hearts we secretly say, "Well, I wish I had not acted that way; and I wish I had not spoken that way. I am sorry about these things." But we do not want to take responsibility for them. Yet it is only when we take responsibility that God will be able to do anything for us.

Psychologists say that anything we are able to envision we are able to accomplish. For instance, if a businessman says, "I want to accomplish a certain goal in business" and he is able to sit down and think it through and focus his mind on it—this very fact means that he is able to accomplish it. If he were not able to accomplish it, he would not be able to set the goal in the first place. This is spiritually true also. If we are able to see something that is wrong about ourselves, we are able to do something about it. We would never be able to recognize the need if we were not able to do something about it. Everything, however, depends on our desire to see what is wrong and on our willingness to acknowledge our responsibility with regard to it. Without this attitude on our part, God cannot work on our behalf.

If God shows us something about our reactions, we can never "unsee" it. The persons closest to us may never know that we saw something of our own needs but God knows this. So we can never truthfully say to God, "Lord, I did not know. I did not see that I was that way." We did see, and God knows that we saw. The only alternatives we have are to hide and try to forget what we have seen or face it realistically and honestly. If we take the responsibility for our reactions and say, "I want God to do something about these reactions of mine. I want Him to strengthen me in this area. I do not want to

continue to be guilty of these reactions. I want to grow. I want to
mature. I want God to be glorified
in my reactions in life"—then God
can help us. We want other people
to take responsibility for their
actions; we must be as quick to
take responsibility for our reactions. If we do not care to take
responsibility, we will remain
miserable. We will live in a dream
world, thinking we are what we are
not. Only as we take responsibility
is there any hope for us.

Now the question arises, How
do we take responsibility? How do
we settle such matters? First of all
we must admit that we have seen
what God is showing us. We must
admit that we have seen what our
reactions have revealed about us. If
we reacted in a critical manner, we
must immediately admit that we
have been critical. No matter what
someone else may have done to us,
the thing we want to do is admit
our wrong reaction. Furthermore,
we must ask the Holy Spirit to
make the matter so real to us that
we clearly see what our need is. So

the first essential is that we admit we have seen what our reactions have revealed about us.

In the second place, we must refuse to excuse and defend ourselves. To defend ourselves is the natural tendency of all of us; but our decision must be "I am not going to defend myself, because someone else has been guilty of wrong actions." We must admit in very simple honesty (which is not an easy thing to do) that this is the way we are. We dare not excuse ourselves nor wait for others to confess their wrong actions first. A wife must not wait for her husband to change his actions before she changes her reactions. The same goes for the husband. We dare not wait for others to change their attitudes before we change ours. Since God has shown us what we are, we take the responsibility and trust the Lord for victory in that particular area, regardless of what anyone else does.

In the third place, we must fully confess our wrong. This does not mean in a casual way: "Oh

Lord, You know I am not perfect, and I could be a little better, so help me to act a little better under the circumstances." No! We must confess, "Lord, I have sinned in my reactions; I was critical and hateful. Lord, I confess that to You and ask You to help me with my reactions."

God's wonderful promises are clear. "If we confess our sins"—and wrong reactions are sins—"he is faithful and just to forgive us our sins, and to cleanse us from all unrighteousness" (I John 1:9). Wonderful! If we confess, fully, God forgives us.

The Apostle Paul said, "I am crucified with Christ: nevertheless I live; yet not I, but Christ liveth in me" (Gal. 2:20). This is the heart of it all. Christ lives in me! What kind of life did He live on earth? What were His reactions? His situations were not always pleasant and advantageous, but how did He react to people in every situation? His reactions can be our reactions if we really let Him live in us. It is not a matter of deciding, "I am going

33

to try to be more like Christ; I am going to try to follow in His steps." It is far more than that, for Christ lives in us who are Christians. Therefore, we ourselves are channels through which He can live. We want His reactions to be our reactions. We know we cannot do it of ourselves. But the Lord who lives within will react in us the same way He reacted when He was here on the earth. This is the secret. No wonder Paul said, "I can do all things through Christ which strengtheneth me" (Phil. 4:13). He is able; He is enough. Let us trust Him to do this.

Chapter 4

Conspicuous Recognition

Chapters 1—3 have dealt with basic principles regarding our reactions. Now let us examine a Bible illustration that shows the far-reaching results of right and wrong reactions. This illustration has to do with the family of Jacob and particularly with his son Joseph.

The narrative of Joseph in the Book of Genesis is not only familiar to many of us, it is also fascinating and full of rich and important lessons. It begins in Genesis 37, when Joseph was 17 years of age, taking care of sheep with his older brothers. In verse 3 we find these words: "Now Israel (Jacob) loved Joseph more than all his children, because he was the son of his old age: and he made him a coat of many colours."

Here is the first reaction we want to examine—Jacob's reaction to Joseph. It is a reaction of conspicuous recognition showing partiality on Jacob's part. He had twelve sons but only the two youngest—Joseph and Benjamin—were born to his favorite wife, Rachel, who died giving birth to Benjamin. Jacob was 91 years of age when Joseph was born, and his partiality to this boy was immediate. Jacob, of course, was old enough to be Joseph's grandfather. So here was a proud, doting, affectionate and sentimental old man, undoubtedly spending much time with Joseph, since by this time the older sons were grown up and working out in the fields. Then, too, Joseph may have reminded him of his own youth. Or Joseph may have resembled his mother, Rachel. Whatever the reason was, the fact stands out in bold relief that Jacob loved Joseph more than all his other children.

Here is undiluted partiality. The conspicuous recognition Jacob accorded Joseph is the beginning of a very sad story. Such parental partiality and favoritism is always foolish and evil. How many family circles have been disrupted because of this common sin. How many individuals have been marred for life because they grew up in an atmosphere of favoritism. Not only was Jacob foolish in being partial, but he was still more foolish in the way he showed it. He did not try to hide it. He made this boy a coat of many colors, actually a long-sleeved garment that showed Jacob intended to transfer the rights of the firstborn to Joseph. So as far as the older brothers were concerned, Joseph was supplanting them. Jacob's partiality and favoritism was proof of this.

Jacob himself was reared in a home where partiality was shown. He was his mother's pet. Together, they conspired to deceive his father, Isaac, and Jacob's older brother, Esau. It seems that partiality must be the sin we are afraid to mention. In all of my years of attending church I have never heard a sermon on partiality. Yet think how much favoritism there is in business. Someone is preferred because he "butters up" the boss, or "shines his shoes." Or a person is promoted, but not for his business merits. This is partly the reason for the saying "It's not what you know but whom you know that really counts."

How about partiality in the church? Someone may be elected to an office or position because of family connections. There are many churches across our land that are controlled by a family clique and where persons are honored because of their relatives. They are honored perhaps because of their financial contributions, while others of lesser means are ignored. Some persons are pushed and promoted, not because of their spiritual qualifications or abilities, but because they know the right people. They shake the right hands. They are careful to vote on the right side. Thus a whole church may be controlled by partiality. What a tragedy!

Listen to what James writes in his epistle: "Dear Brothers, how can you claim that you belong to the Lord Jesus Christ, the Lord of glory, if you show favoritism to rich people and look down on poor people? If a man comes into your church dressed in expensive clothes and with valuable gold rings on his fingers, and at the same moment another man comes in who is poor and dressed in threadbare clothes, and you make a lot of fuss over the rich man and give him the best seat in the house and say to the poor man, 'You can stand over there if you like, or else sit on the floor'— well, . . . you are guided by wrong motives" (James 2:1-4, Living Bible). "If ye have respect [prejudice or favoritism] to persons, ye commit sin" (v. 9). These are strong and pointed words regarding this very common sin!

Partiality, of course, does its deadliest work in home and family relations. It is always disastrous when a child suspects that his parent is not fair. A favorite child is likely to become smug and complacent, while the less favored one tends to become discouraged and morose. Never in a home and family should comparisons be made concerning the children. Yet, many of us parents are guilty of comparing one with another, and one child's accomplishments with another's lack of accomplishments. Nothing so destroys initiative and encourages a feeling of inferiority in an individual as comparing him unfavorably with someone else.

In fact, the Bible says we should never compare ourselves with others, because this is not wise. Neither then should we ever compare our children with other children in the family or outside the family. How often one child is recognized for accomplishment but another is neglected. One child is shown affection but another is overlooked. One child is complimented while another child is criticized. One child is disciplined while another is allowed to run wild. Each child has certain strengths of character. Each one excels in some area. And each child must receive unconditional love.

A parent should not state he or she loves a child because the child's behaviour is good. Yet so often we hear, "If you are not a good boy, Mother will not love you." A child must have unconditional love. A parent should not love a child simply because the child makes the parent feel good by what he does. This is making a child responsible for an adult's happiness. A child dare not be neglected by his mother because he has some undesirable trait that her own husband may have or because the child reminds her of a relative whom she does not like. A child must be loved for his own sake. His own God-given personality should be developed impartially. This is what helps make parenthood such a creative opportunity, because each child is different.

I have noticed that each of my own boys is different. Yet each must be loved. Each one has a soul and a life to be used for God. Each one demands personal and particular understanding. What a wonderful challenge to be a parent in these days!

Visit a prison and ask the prisoners how many of them grew up in a home where they felt that they were the black sheep of the family. You will be amazed at their answers. Some prisoners have this motto tattooed on their bodies: "Born to lose." In other words, their whole life has been a life of feeling inferior, unwanted and worthless, often because of neglect or partiality in the home.

We learned that after the Korean War, 21 GI's went over to the enemy. They decided to surrender their American citizenship and defect to Communism. A study of these men and their backgrounds revealed that 19 of them had felt unloved and unwanted by their father or their stepfather at home. Nineteen of the 21 had come out of homes where they felt unloved and unwanted. Sixteen of these had withdrawn into themselves. Eighteen of the 21 took no part in any school activities or sports, and only one of the 21 was ever chosen by his classmates for anything. How revealing this study is. It shows us that there was a basic failure at home as far as all these young men were concerned. They were not given the impartial and the unconditional love and encouragement that they needed from their parents. So family failure is a basic failure, and it shows itself in other areas of life.

Sin first came into the home. Sin first showed its ugly head at the home and family level—Adam and Eve in the Garden of Eden. It is at the home level that the Devil does his deadliest work. If he can defeat us at home, he has defeated us all along the line. If he can defeat our children at home, he will defeat them in every area of life. This is why we must be so careful of our reactions to our children at home. We must never be guilty of reacting toward one by giving him conspicuous recognition and thereby downgrading the others.

43

Jacob's reaction was wrong. Parental partiality is always wrong. That we must never forget.

I talked some time ago with a young lady in a midwestern state. She told me through her blinding tears how she was raised in a home of favoritism and partiality. She said, "My sister was better looking than me. Her hair was prettier than mine. She looked better in every way and had more ability and more boyfriends. She had a more active social life. Everybody recognized her. Visitors would come to our home and remark about my sister, but I was neglected and forgotten."

Finally she said, "I have done so many strange and awful things—just to get attention." She added, "I have tried everything. I have committed many sins just to get some kind of attention from boys and from other people."

We say, "Well, what a tragedy!"

Yes, but whose fault is this? We cannot blame the girl entirely. Her parents share the greater blame because of their favoritism and partiality. They did not teach this girl that she was important and that she was valuable to God, to them and to the world. They did not teach her to know that she had a contribution to make that her sister could never make.

Yes, Jacob was wrong in showing parental partiality. And we must be careful to see that our reaction is not as his was, or our children will suffer, and God's plan for them may be thwarted.

Chapter 5

Consequences of Partiality

In the preceding chapter we saw from Genesis 37 that Jacob reacted to Joseph by giving him conspicuous recognition. This was a reaction of partiality. We will now consider some of the consequences of that partiality.

Jacob's sons reacted with hostility to his reaction to Joseph. This is understandable when we know human nature as the Bible shows it to be. Whenever someone is favored in a family, the other members of the family react—usually with opposition to the one favored. Joseph's brothers reacted against him with cruel rejection.

"And when his brethren saw that their father loved him more than all his brethren, they hated him, and could not speak peaceably unto him. And Joseph dreamed a dream, and he told it his brethren: and they hated him yet the more" (Gen. 37:4,5). In verse 11 we learn that they envied him; and verse 18 tells us that they conspired against him to kill him.

The events followed each other rapidly. Jacob was partial to his son Joseph and loved him more than all his other sons. When the brothers saw this, they turned on Joseph with hatred and hostility. Then, to make matters worse, Joseph recounted a dream God had given him. He said to his brothers, in effect, "I had a dream in which God showed me that someday I would rule over you, and that you would bow the knee to me."

Joseph may have been unwise in relating this dream, but his motives were not wrong. He was not seeking to exalt himself. But his telling it only added to the hostility that was building up in the hearts of his brothers. This, remember, was in addition to the fact that his father had given him a coat that signified Jacob's special affection for him.

No wonder they hated Joseph when they saw him wearing his special coat. But this was not all. He had also brought home a report of the evil actions of his older brothers. It is not hard to see why they built up resentment and hatred in their hearts toward him.

So their reaction was one of cruel rejection. Rejection is the natural reaction to partiality. The one favored becomes the one hated. Hostility springs from envy and jealousy. This shows the folly and the evil of parental favoritism. It provoked hatred in Jacob's family where there should have been love. And it was this hatred that made the brothers decide, "We'll take care of him!"

As the narrative progresses, we learn that Joseph was sent out to see his brothers as they were taking care of the sheep. They made him prisoner and were going to kill him, but they put him down into a pit instead. Ultimately they sold him as a slave to some traders who were going down to Egypt. No doubt, their thinking was something like this: "It serves him right. He shouldn't have the coat anyway. We'll rip it off him. He's the boy that said he's going to be exalted above us. We'll show him. We'll put him beneath us. He's the one who told tales about us. We'll take care of him for good. We'll put a little common sense and reality into his head."

Resentful and bitter, and like any of us guilty of wrongdoing, the brothers did not find it hard to justify their wicked reactions. They possibly said, "We had reasons for the way we felt. If our father had not shown such favoritism, and if this boy had not been so foolish, we wouldn't have acted in that way. So it really wasn't our fault; it was their own fault. We had good reason for what we did."

But we can never justify hatred. We can never justify resentment. There is no way in the world that we can justify bitterness and hostility. In the case of Joseph's brothers, these things almost ended in murder.

We always think that we have reasons for the way we react at times. There may even be other situations that contribute to our difficulty. But we can never justify a wrong reaction before God. If I hate someone, that reaction is wrong regardless of how it has been provoked. If I have become resentful and bitter and unforgiving toward someone, I can never justify that attitude no matter what that person may have done to provoke me.

I remember many years ago that a well-known man of God and I had a bitter disagreement. We disagreed on several matters, and he was as strong-willed about them as I was. He told me very frankly how he felt and what he thought about me. And I told him very frankly how I felt and what I thought about him.

We were both bitter. We were both resentful. We were both envious. And I went away thinking, "Well, I have reasons for feeling this way. I can justify my reactions. After all, he started it. He's older than I am. He expressed hatred first. And I have good reasons—and if he hadn't done this and said this, then I wouldn't have reacted in this way." Finally God got me to the place where He could show me this. Then I had to go back to this man and say to him (the hardest thing I have ever had to do in my life), "I am wrong; my reactions are wrong. Regardless of what anyone else has said or done, my reactions have been wrong, and I cannot justify them." Only then was I free. Only then did I have victory.

To my great surprise this dear man turned to me and said, "And my reactions were wrong, too. I am also guilty."

We became fast friends, because we were honest with each other. We did not seek to blame each other for our reactions, but we faced them honestly and took responsibility for them.

Joseph's brothers had a reaction of cruel rejection. Maybe we have had such a reaction. Maybe there has been hatred in our hearts toward someone else. This cannot be justified. Let us confess it to God and make it right with that other person. Then let us decide that regardless of how anyone else acts toward us, our reactions are going to be right in the sight of God.

This whole story of Joseph is a series of reactions to reactions. So consider now Joseph's reaction to the rejection of his brothers. He reacted with creative resignation.

A person's real character is revealed by his reaction when he has been misunderstood, mistreated or hated. If we react in the same way others have reacted—with criticism and hostility, then we are no better than they are. And we are as guilty as they. We need to confess our sinful reactions to God just as much as they need to confess theirs. Our reactions can ruin us as much as their reactions can ruin them.

If we react by becoming discouraged and fretful, and give in to feelings of inferiority and self-rejection, we are also being ruined. Any wrong reaction is ruinous. If

from this never to trust people again. Even one's best friends can deceive him. If I could just get out of here and get back home!"

No such negative talk! He never whined; he never murmured. His attitude was victorious and positive: "Here I am. I never dreamed I would be in such a predicament. But I am here, and it looks like I'll be here for a long time. This was not my choosing. God allowed this. God must have something in mind for me. I'll find out what it is. However long I must stay in Egypt, this experience will further my training and be a stepping-stone in my life. I will do my best and trust God for the outcome."

What a man! A man like this cannot be hurt. Everything serves him. Everyone helps him. What is more, God blesses and prospers him.

Some people always want to go back home. They want out of any new situation that presents problems and difficulties they do not understand. They want to get back to familiar ground. Actually they do not want change. They do not want the opportunities that every situation provides to bring about their maturity. They lack creative resignation. But this was the quality Joseph had. This must be our reaction in every difficulty.

Chapter 6

Tested and Exalted

Joseph's reaction of creative resignation enabled God to prosper him personally in his situation. It also enabled God to bless and prosper the entire house of Potiphar. This was because Joseph's relationship to God and to his difficulty was right. God prospered the Egyptian and all of his interests because Joseph had the right attitude. Joseph was God's channel of blessing in that situation. This is true today. Husbands and wives will find that their entire home can be blessed if they have the right relationship to God, the right attitude in their situation, and the right reaction to their difficulties. They can be the channel of blessing and prosperity to their entire home and family.

This does not mean that if a person is serving the Lord faithfully and honoring Him in his reactions, there will be no future problems. Joseph's experience is proof of this. A great temptation came to him right in the midst of his spiritual prosperity and service. According to Genesis 39:6 he was "a goodly person and well favoured." He was not only a handsome young man, he also had an attractive personality. In addition, he was a man of many talents and abilities. This drew Potiphar's wife's attention to him. She cast her eyes upon him and decided she would entice him to sin.

It is no problem to entice someone who is already living on a low, shallow level. But here was a man of honesty and integrity; here was a man who had been unusually blessed of God.

Possibly she tried to overcome his scruples by suggesting, "Surely you can have a little fun. Don't be so inflexible in your standards. No one will ever know about this. Stolen waters are sweet, Joseph, and bread eaten in secret places is pleasant."

Mark keenly the strong reaction of this young man Joseph. What a contrast to this day of so-called sexual freedom, this time of loose morals, this day of the so-called new morality. It was a reaction of courageous refusal. The Bible says in Genesis 39:8: "But he refused." How clear and simple and strong and definite that is.

Let us learn several important lessons right here about temptation and our meeting it. Number one: temptation comes to all people—to any person in any land. Here was Joseph, a leader in Potiphar's house in charge of all of his possessions, and here was Potiphar's wife, also a person of prominence. But whether prominent or lowly, temptation comes to all. Wherever we are, whatever our position: husband or wife or child or pastor or missionary; whatever the place: in the home or business or church— temptation comes to all. It knows no strangers. Everyone who is alive is tempted. If we have a mind with which we think, there will be temptation through that mind. If we have a body in which we live, there will be temptation through that body. Everyone alive is tempted in this life and always will be. Temptation is our lifelong companion; therefore, temptation should never come as a surprise. Everyone is tempted, whatever his situation, whatever his station in life, whatever his relationship to God. Temptation comes to all. Settle this once and for all.

The second is this: temptation comes during spiritual prosperity and often follows a great victory. Joseph had been serving the Lord and was busy and prosperous. The Bible says of him that God's hand was upon him and God's hand was upon the entire house because of Joseph. Then, right in the midst of this prosperity, while he was enjoying the rich blessing of God, this violent temptation came.

We find this principle illustrated all through the Bible. There was Elijah's great victory at Mount Carmel. He stood for God in the face of all the opposition from the king and the false prophets of Baal. Right after this notable victory he gave way to despair and discouragement. He was driven into the wilderness by a threat from a woman. So, after a great victory on the mountain, there was a great temptation in the valley. The same was true after David had killed the giant Goliath. Everyone was singing David's praises, and this made Saul jealous. He wanted to kill David. Here again, right after a God-given victory, a great testing arose for David.

Daniel was exalted to the position of prime minister of Babylon. God honored and blessed him in every way, even giving him the confidence of the king. Then, right in the midst of this prosperity and success, he was falsely accused and thrown into the lions' den. After the victory came the testing.

In the case of our Lord Jesus Christ—when was His great testing? Right after He was filled with the Spirit; immediately after the Spirit of God anointed Him for His ministry. It was then that He was led into the wilderness to be tested of the Devil. The greatest testing followed the greatest victory.

Paul and Silas saw God working in a tremendous way through their ministry. But right in the midst of their spiritual success they were beaten, hauled off to prison and left to languish in the stocks. Spiritual prosperity was followed by serious problems. Mark this fact: The most dangerous times in our lives can be right after a thrilling spiritual victory.

Third, we must remember that temptation often comes from unexpected sources. The Devil uses anyone he can in any situation. Joseph minded his own business, and the very person he should have been able to trust was the one who tried to entice him.

The fourth thing to remember is that temptation is continuous. It is repeated. It is persistent. The Bible says Potiphar's wife tempted Joseph one day and he refused. Then she approached him another day, and finally it was a daily enticement. Daily she begged him. She did not let up. Yet daily he was firm in his refusal. So we must learn that victory over temptation one day does not mean there will be no temptations the next day. Every day we live we will face temptations of one kind or another, often the same kind. Temptation will be our lifelong companion. But every day Jesus Christ can enable us to have the right reaction to stand strong and to courageously refuse.

Consider more closely Joseph's reaction. In the first place he was simple and firm in his answer. He said, "No, I cannot do this." He did not argue with her. He did not discuss the matter. There was no equivocation, no hesitancy. He did not say, "Well, let's talk this over and let me try to convince you that this is not a wise thing to do at this time. Very simply and courageously he refused and said, "This is wrong." His reaction was clear and strong on the side of righteousness.

In the second place, this passage in Genesis teaches us that he feared sin, not the temptation. So many of us Christians have a fatalistic dread of testing. We often think, If I weren't tested so often, life would be so much easier. But we must never fear trials. We should fear sin only. Testing is a wonderful blessing. It has many beneficial effects. Were it not for frequent testings our souls would become weak and lifeless. So we ought to thank God for testings and to fear only sin.

Joseph did not seek temptation nor make provision for it. But when temptation came in the line of duty and service, he was ready to face it. He considered every temptation a stepping-stone to victory. He considered every temptation an opportunity to defeat the Devil. Napoleon said, "He who fears being conquered is sure of defeat." So Joseph feared sin but not the trial.

In the third place, Joseph knew that sin was against God. So he said to this woman, "How then can I do this great wickedness, and sin against God?" (Gen. 39:9). He would have sinned against his own body. Every act of immorality is against our own body, the Bible says. He would also have sinned against this woman and against her husband and family. But Joseph knew that sin is primarily and essentially against God. So uncompromisingly he said, "I cannot do this and sin against God."

Fourth, He was determined to be victorious at any cost. Here was a young man who had decided: "I don't care what happens to me. This woman may lie about me, she may accuse me, I may lose my position and my reputation and I may be confined to prison." All these things happened. But he determined in his heart: "I am going to maintain my integrity. I am not going to jeopardize my relationship to God. My reaction is going to be clear, strong, and without hesitation for what is right."

Consider now Joseph's reaction to his erring brethren after he was made the prime minister of Egypt. His brothers came down to Egypt to get corn because there was a famine in the land. They stood before Joseph but did not recognize him. What was his reaction to them? How did he respond in the light of all that they had done to him?

His reaction was one of godly retaliation. He could have thought, Now I am in a position to get even. I have my brothers just where I want them, and I am going to make them pay for their sins. I am going to let them know that the dreams I had about my being exalted above them were really true. This is the fulfillment. I am going to show these men that they cannot do what they did to me and get by with it. I am going to get my revenge.

No. Not one fleeting thought of this kind seemed to cross his mind. Instead, he said to them, "God did send me before you to preserve life. So now it was not you that sent me hither, but God: and he hath made me a father to Pharoah, and lord of all his house" (Gen. 45:5,8). Joseph assured them that he wanted them near him and urged them to move to Egypt. Forgiveness! This was his godly retaliation: forgiveness and love!

Joseph said that their deception was turned by God into good for him. His problems were his opportunities. His persecutors were unwittingly his friends. Everything that happened to him furthered God's plans and lifted and strengthened him. He was not hurt, for God brought good out of evil. God was in it all, so Joseph forgave them and wanted to love and help them.

Joseph counted no man his enemy. He made them his friends, because he had the right reactions. Is this how we react? Joseph was a genuine and mature believer. He experienced the truth of Romans 8:28 centuries before it was written: "All things work together for good to them that love God, to them who are the called according to his purpose." Joseph believed, as Jesus our Lord later said, that we are to love our enemies. We do not say that we have no enemies, but *we* are not *their* enemies. We will love them. This is the right reaction. This is gloriously possible as we allow the Lord to control us. Let us forgive and love when we are wronged; embrace these as opportunities for maturity, and God will prosper us increasingly.

Back to the Bible is a nonprofit ministry dedicated to Bible teaching, evangelism and edification of Christians worldwide.

If we may assist you in knowing more about Christ and the Christian life, please write to us without obligation:

Back to the Bible
P.O. Box 82808
Lincoln, NE 68501